D0757681

WITHDRAWN

NEW WESTMINSTER PUBLIC LIBRARY

C\

Firefighter

CAREERS WITH CHARACTER

CAREERS WITH CHARACTER

Firefighter

John Riddle and Rae Simons

Mason Crest

Mason Crest
450 Parkway Drive, Suite D
Broomall, PA 19008
www.masoncrest.com

Copyright © 2014 by Mason Crest, an imprint of National Highlights, Inc. All rights reserved. No part of this publication may be reproduced or transmitted in any form or by any means, electronic or mechanical, including photocopying, recording, taping or any information storage and retrieval system, without permission from the publisher.

Printed in the Hashemite Kingdom of Jordan.

First printing
9 8 7 6 5 4 3 2 1

Series ISBN: 978-1-4222-2750-3
ISBN: 978-1-4222-2756-5
ebook ISBN: 978-1-4222-9052-1

The Library of Congress has cataloged the
hardcopy format(s) as follows:

Library of Congress Cataloging-in-Publication Data

Riddle, John.
  Firefighter / John Riddle and Rae Simons.
    pages cm. – (Careers with character)
  Audience: Grade 7 to 8.
  Includes index.
  ISBN 978-1-4222-2756-5 (hardcover : alk. paper) – ISBN 978-1-4222-2750-3 (series) – ISBN 978-1-4222-9052-1 (ebook)
  1. Fire fighters–Juvenile literature. [1. Fire extinction–Juvenile literature. 2. Vocational guidance.] I. Simons, Rae, 1957- II. Title.
  HD8039.F5R53 2014
  363.37023–dc23
                          2013007501

Produced by Vestal Creative Services.
www.vestalcreative.com

Photo Credits:
Corel: pp. 10, 13, 16, 17, 19, 21, 24, 26, 28, 32, 34, 35, 36, 37, 40, 42, 43, 44, 58, 61, 62, 63, 64, 65, 68, 70, 72, 73, 76, 78, 79, 84, 86
PhotoDisc: pp. 14, 27, 82

The individuals in these images are models, and the images are for illustrative purposes only. To the best knowledge of the publisher, all other images are in the public domain. If any image has been inadvertently uncredited or miscredited, please notify Vestal Creative Services, Vestal, New York 13850, so that rectification can be made for future printings.

CONTENTS

We each leave a fingerprint on the world.
Our careers are the work we do in life.
Our characters are shaped by the choices
we make to do good.
When we combine careers with character,
we touch the world with power.

INTRODUCTION

by Dr. Cheryl Gholar
and Dr. Ernestine G. Riggs

In today's world, the awesome task of choosing or staying in a career has become more involved than one would ever have imagined in past decades. Whether the job market is robust or the demand for workers is sluggish, the need for top-performing employees with good character remains a priority on most employers' lists of "must have" or "must keep." When critical decisions are being made regarding a company or organization's growth or future, job performance and work ethic are often the determining factors as to who will remain employed and who will not.

How does one achieve success in one's career and in life? Victor Frankl, the Austrian psychologist, summarized the concept of success in the preface to his book *Man's Search for Meaning* as: "The unintended side-effect of one's personal dedication to a course greater than oneself." Achieving value by responding to life and careers from higher levels of knowing and being is a specific goal of teaching and learning in "Careers with Character." What constitutes success for us as individuals can be found deep within our belief system. Seeking, preparing, and attaining an excellent career that aligns with our personality is an outstanding goal. However, an excellent career augmented by exemplary character is a visible expression of the human need to bring meaning, purpose, and value to our work.

Career education informs us of employment opportunities, occupational outlooks, earnings, and preparation needed to perform certain tasks. Character education provides insight into how a person of good character might choose to respond, initiate an action, or perform specific tasks in the presence of an ethical dilemma. "Careers with Character" combines the two and teaches students that careers are more than just jobs. Career development is incomplete without character development. What better way to explore careers and character than to make them a single package to be opened, examined, and reflected upon as a means of understanding the greater whole of who we are and what work can mean when one chooses to become an employee of character?

Character can be defined simply as "who you are even when no one else is around." Your character is revealed by your choices and actions. These bear your personal signature, validating the story of who you are. They are the fingerprints you leave behind on the people you meet and know; they are the ideas you bring into reality. Your choices tell the world what you truly believe.

Character, when viewed as a standard of excellence, reminds us to ask ourselves when choosing a career: "Why this particular career, for what purpose, and to what end?" The authors of "Careers with Character" knowledgeably and passionately, through their various vignettes, enable one to experience an inner journey that is both intellectual and moral. Students will find themselves, when confronting decisions in real life, more prepared, having had experiential learning opportunities through this series. The books, however, do not separate or negate the individual good from the academic skills or intellect needed to perform the required tasks that lead to productive career development and personal fulfillment.

Each book is replete with exemplary role models, practical strategies, instructional tools, and applications. In each volume, individuals of character work toward ethical leadership, learning how to respond appropriately to issues of not only right versus wrong, but issues of right versus right, understanding the possible benefits and consequences of their decisions. A wealth of examples is provided.

What is it about a career that moves our hearts and minds toward fulfilling a dream? It is our character. The truest approach to finding out who we are and what illuminates our lives is to look within. At the very heart of career development is good character. At the heart of good character is an individual who knows and loves the good, and seeks to share the good with others. By exploring careers and character together, we create internal and external environments that support and enhance each other, challenging students to lead conscious lives of personal quality and true richness every day.

Is there a difference between doing the right thing, and doing things right? Career questions ask, "What do you know about a specific career?" Character questions ask, "Now that you know about a specific career, what will you choose to do with what you know?" "How will you perform certain tasks and services for others, even when no one else is around?" "Will all individuals be given your best regardless of their socioeconomic background, physical condition, ethnicity, or religious beliefs?" Character questions often challenge the authenticity of what we say we believe and value in the workplace and in our personal lives.

Character and career questions together challenge us to pay attention to our lives and not fall asleep on the job. Career knowledge, self-knowledge, and ethical wisdom help us answer deeper questions about the meaning of work; they give us permission to transform our lives. Personal integrity is the price of admission.

The insight of one "ordinary" individual can make a difference in the world—if that one individual believes that character is an amazing gift to uncap knowledge and talents to empower the human community. Our world needs everyday heroes in the workplace—and "Careers with Character" challenges students to become those heroes.

Firefighters need to be people of character to face the dangers of their job.

JOB REQUIREMENTS

Success in life depends on the choices you make.

CHAPTER ONE

A t three o'clock in the morning the firefighters are sleeping soundly in their bunks at the firehouse. The past two nights have been quiet, with no emergencies. But suddenly an emergency *dispatcher* takes a telephone call; a woman is calling frantically to report that the house across the street from her is on fire. "Hurry!" she screams. "Send the fire department now!" At the same time the emergency operator is taking the information about the call, he is pushing a button that sends the fire department an emergency alarm.

As the alarm blares throughout the fire station, the sleeping firefighters spring into action. Within 90 seconds the two fire engines

In the Phoenix, Arizona, Fire Department, Chief Alan Brunacini believes that everyone needs to be able to make good decisions, and in order to accomplish that, they must have high moral character. The chief must be able to depend on the firefighters that are on the job to make decisions that will affect life or death and the destruction of property. In order to make the firefighters' jobs a little easier, Chief Brunacini gives each firefighter a small card that asks these questions.

- Is it the right thing for the customer?
- Is it the right thing for our department?
- Is it legal, ethical, and nice?
- Is it safe?
- Is it on your organizational level?
- Is it something you are willing to be accountable for?
- Is it consistent with our department's values and policies?

If the answer is yes to all these questions, don't ask for permission, just do it!

are racing toward the scene of the house fire. By the time they pull up in front of the house, only ten minutes have gone by since the fire actually began. In this case someone had fallen asleep with the fireplace still burning—and failed to notice a burning ember that made its way onto the carpet. The occupants of the house all escaped unharmed and now stand at the end of their driveway, watching as the firefighters battle the blaze.

Before long the crew has the fire under control, and a few minutes later it is officially declared out. The damage to the house has been minimal, and no lives were lost or injuries reported. The firefighters spend the next hour watching to make sure the fire does not restart. Once the chief is certain it is safe, the fire crew begins to put away their hoses and other equipment to return to the fire station.

Firefighters need to be able to work with others and develop a strong sense of team spirit.

"Another job well done," the chief says to his fire-fighting crew. The firefighters feel good about the job they have done; they are proud to be able to serve their community.

Many children have fantasies where they take part in scenarios like this one. They dream about becoming a firefighter when they grow up. In school they learn about how brave the firefighters are and how they risk their lives to save the lives of innocent people. However, by the time most people reach high school, other career choices and decisions usually replace those childhood dreams.

One way to see if a career in fire fighting is right for you is to become a member of a volunteer fire-fighting company. In most communities, you must be at least 16 years old to join.

Fires caused by gasoline can be particularly hazardous.

Most people in a community, however, are still aware of the fire department that serves them. When they hear a siren or see a fire engine racing toward a fire, they are reminded of the firefighters and how they are called to serve. Many of us often take for granted the work these brave men and women perform. But ever since September 11, 2001, when jet planes were crashed into American buildings, the whole world has come to realize the importance of firefighters. We have a better appreciation for the many heroic deeds they perform day in and day out.

Every year, fires and other emergencies take thousands of lives and destroy property worth billions of dollars. Firefighters help protect the public against these dangers by rapidly responding to a variety of emergencies. They are frequently the first emergency personnel at the scene of a traffic accident or medical emergency and

The International Association of Firefighters has created a Firefighter Code of Ethics to help firefighters remember their career mission and goals:

As a firefighter and member of the International Association of Firefighters, my fundamental duty is to serve humanity; to safeguard and preserve life and property against the elements of fire and disaster; and maintain a proficiency in the art and science of fire engineering.

I will uphold the standards of my profession, continually search for new and improved methods and share my knowledge and skills with my contemporaries and descendants.

I will never allow personal feelings, nor danger to self, deter me from my responsibilities as a firefighter.

I will at all times respect the property and rights of all men and women, the laws of my community and my country, and the chosen way of life of my fellow citizens.

I recognize the badge of my office as a symbol of public faith, and I accept it as a public trust to be held so long as I am true to the ethics of the fire service. I will constantly strive to achieve the objectives and ideals, dedicating myself to my chosen profession—saving of life, fire prevention and fire suppression.

As a member of the International Association of Firefighters, I accept this self-imposed and self-enforced obligation as my responsibility.

may be called upon to put out a fire, treat injuries, or perform other vital functions.

Firefighters work in a variety of settings, including urban and suburban areas, airports, chemical plants, other industrial sites, and rural areas like grasslands and forests. In addition, some firefighters work in *hazardous materials units* that are trained for the control, prevention, and cleanup of oil spills and other hazardous materials incidents.

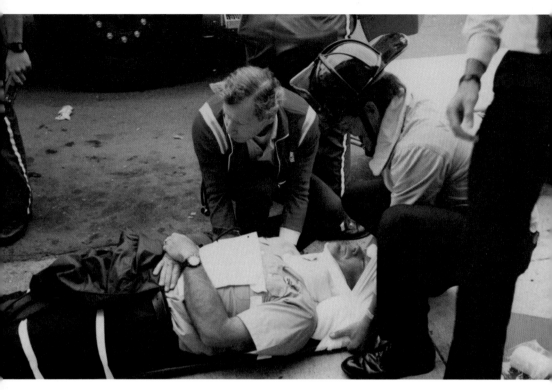

Volunteer firefighters often provide emergency medical services as well.

Firefighters have assumed a range of responsibilities, including emergency medical services. In fact, most calls to which firefighters respond involve medical emergencies, and about half of all fire departments provide ambulance service for victims. Firefighters receive training in emergency medical procedures, and many fire departments require them to be certified as emergency medical technicians.

During duty hours, firefighters must be prepared to respond immediately to a fire or any other emergency that arises. Because fighting fires is dangerous and complex, it requires organization and teamwork. At every emergency scene, firefighters perform specific duties assigned by a superior officer. At fires, they connect hose lines to hydrants, operate a pump to send water to high-pressure hoses, and position ladders to enable workers to deliver water to the fire. They also rescue victims and provide emergency medical attention as needed, ventilate smoke-filled areas, and attempt to salvage the contents of buildings. Their duties may change several times while the company is in action. Sometimes they remain at the site of a disaster for days at a time, rescuing trapped survivors and assisting with medical treatment.

Between alarms, firefighters clean and maintain equipment, conduct practice drills and fire inspections, and participate in physical fitness activities. They also prepare written reports on fire incidents and review fire science literature to keep abreast of technological developments and changing administrative practices and policies.

Applicants for municipal fire-fighting jobs generally must meet several requirements:

- a written exam;
- tests of strength, physical stamina, coordination, and agility;
- and a medical examination that includes drug screening.

After a car accident, firefighters are often the first on the scene.

18

Firefighters don't only put out fires. Many are also trained to be part of search and rescue efforts. This means they often work with *canine search teams* and use listening devices to help them find survivors. They learn to dismantle buildings quickly to find people trapped in rubble. Especially since attacks such as the bombing at Oklahoma City in 1995 and the September 11, 2001 terrorist attacks, more and more fire-fighting crews are ready to help people in the event of a terrorist attack or other disaster.

Workers may be monitored on a random basis for drug use after accepting employment. Examinations are generally open to persons who are at least 18 years of age and have a high school education or the equivalent. Those who receive the highest scores in all phases of testing have the best chances for appointment. The completion of community college courses in fire science may improve an applicant's chances for appointment. In recent years, an increasing proportion of entrants to this occupation has had some post-secondary education.

A number of fire departments have accredited apprenticeship programs lasting up to five years. These programs combine formal, technical instruction with on-the-job training under the supervision of experienced firefighters. Technical instruction covers subjects such as fire-fighting techniques and equipment, chemical hazards associated with various combustible building materials, emergency medical procedures, and fire prevention and safety. Fire departments frequently conduct training programs, and some firefighters attend training sessions sponsored by the U.S. National Fire Academy. These training sessions cover topics including executive development, anti-*arson* techniques, disaster preparedness, hazardous materials control, and public fire safety and education. Some states also have extensive firefighter training and certification programs. In addition, a number of colleges and universities offer courses leading to two- or four-year degrees in fire engineering or fire science. Many fire departments offer firefighters incentives such as tuition reimbursement or higher pay for completing advanced training.

A firefighter needs to possess good character qualities. These come by choice, not by accident or coincidence.

20

Today's firefighters use a variety of trucks.

- Aerial ladder trucks carry telescopic ladders that can stretch up to 135 feet (41 meters).
- Aerial platform trucks use a hydraulic boom to lift a bucket up to 203 feet (62 meters) in the air.
- Rapid Intervention Vehicles are smaller and faster than the other trucks. They can accelerate from 0 to 70 mph as fast as any race car, and they carry enough foam and water to last five minutes—until the other, bigger trucks arrive on the scene.
- Special Equipment Vehicles have special cameras to "see" through thick smoke; cutting equipment that can slice through a car like a can opener; patches for leaking containers of hazardous material; traffic cones; emergency lights; rakes and shovels; and breathing apparatus.
- Crash Rescue Vehicles are especially designed for airport fires. These enormous trucks weigh up to 71 tons and carry seven times as much water and foam as a city pumper truck. They come equipped with telescopic floodlights and a triple extension ladder that's long enough to reach airplane wings.

But to be a good firefighter, you need more than any training program can offer. Working as a firefighter is a team situation, and every member of the team is responsible for the well-being of one another. The ability to work as a member of a team and perform the serious individual responsibilities that come with this type of work is essential. To work as a firefighter you must also be disciplined and organized. You must have the ability to take and carry out orders as necessary. Physical fitness and stamina are essential as well, due to the demanding nature of this work. Firefighters must be fit enough to respond immediately to many differing physical challenges using

Our communities are safer because firefighters possess courage, self-discipline, and citizenship.

equipment in a wide range of circumstances. Emotionally, firefighters need to be *resilient*, often finding themselves in situations where death and serious injury are at close hand; they need to be able to remain calm and make quick decisions under extreme pressure. Good communication skills are required to be able to communicate effectively with colleagues, often in dangerous situations, in a manner that is concise and clear. A sympathetic and understanding manner, as well as good verbal skills, are required when working with members of the public who may be injured and in a state of shock.

In short, firefighters need personal qualities like mental alertness, self-discipline, courage, mechanical aptitude, endurance, strength, and a sense of citizenship or public service. *Initiative* and good judgment are also extremely important, because firefighters need to make quick decisions in emergencies. Because members of a crew live and work closely together under conditions of stress and danger for extended periods, they must be responsible and able to get along well with others. Leadership qualities are necessary for officers, who must establish and maintain discipline and efficiency, as well as direct the activities of firefighters in their companies.

Some of these qualities may be aspects of the personality with which a person was born, but others—like courage, self-discipline, and citizenship—depend more on the choices an individual makes. Every fire department in the country has its own guidelines and requirements for becoming a member of its company. Along with the physical and educational requirements, those fire departments are also seeking candidates that are of high moral character.

Character education expert Tom Lickona believes good character depends on possessing certain core values. We have mentioned a few of these values already—self-discipline, responsibility, courage, and citizenship. Other aspects of good character include integrity and trustworthiness, justice and fairness. These values are more than just coincidental aspects of human personality. They are based on commitment and determination. Living out these values in our personal and professional lives is not only good for us as individuals; it is also good for the world around us. When we demonstrate these qualities in our lives, then we treat others the way we would each like to be treated. And by doing so, we help others, and we make the world a better place for ourselves and others.

Each time a firefighter chooses to be a person of character, he or she often faces a moral choice, sometimes called an *ethical dilemma*. In the chapters that follow, we will see how these character choices are played out in firefighters' lives.

Character is better than ancestry, and personal conduct is of more importance than the highest parentage.

—Thomas John Barnardo

Firefighters are called on to do their jobs at all hours of the day and night.

INTEGRITY AND TRUSTWORTHINESS

Being a person of integrity means you don't tell lies ... even to yourself.

CHAPTER TWO

I n the early morning hours on a bitter cold day in December at a fire station in Ottawa, Canada, the radio suddenly crackled to life and the dispatcher's voice woke the sleeping firefighters. They were professionals who slept in their clothes, ready to get up at all hours to answer a call for help. This time was no different. However, when they realized that the emergency dispatcher was reporting an apartment fire at a high-rise complex that was famous for its false alarms, they probably thought to themselves, *It's just another hoax.*

The fire chief could have easily said to his crew, "Hey, look, it's freezing outside and it's probably just another false alarm, so let's not send all the trucks right away." But even though they had been

The dispatcher immediately passes along any fire reports to the fire station.

called for no reason to that same apartment complex at least two dozen times over the past two months, they still treated this emergency alarm call with the same dedication and enthusiasm they would any other fire alarm. Firefighters know it is their job to answer the call and go where they are needed.

A Definition

If you have integrity, people can trust you. They know you don't lie and that you seek always to be honest, even with yourself. You face up to the facts, even when they are uncomfortable.

So the men and women from that fire station in Ottawa ignored the freezing temperatures and the early hour; they put on their equipment, snatched up the printout the dispatcher had sent their printer, and raced to the scene. When they turned the corner and could see the apartment complex, they knew it was no false alarm this time. The flames were already engulfing the building, and they could see people running out of their apartments still in their nightclothes.

By the time the first few firefighters entered the burning building, it was already filled with heavy black smoke. Some of the firefighters at-

When an engine company rolls to a fire, the crew usually consists of at least six men and women. The chauffeur drives the trucks. "Truckies" ride the fire trucks; they have two jobs: rescue and control the direction of the fire. The fire chief wears a white hat so the crew can recognize him or her even when conditions are dark or smoky. Each member of the fire company crew works just as hard as every member on the scene.

A "truckie" helps control the direction of the fire.

In the course of their work, firefighters are often faced with ethical dilemmas.

tacked the flames while others searched on their hands and knees for anyone trapped inside. One of the firemen located an apartment door that was locked and used his *Halligan bar* to break in. As soon as the firefighters were able to safely enter the apartment, they began looking for victims, marking each doorway with a white X once it had been searched. One firefighter felt several bodies on the floor in front of him and radioed for assistance. Seconds later, two other firefighters joined him and they carried out the survivors, who were choking and gasping for breath. One of them, a woman, was trying to say something to the firefighters. They realized she was screaming, "My baby!" over and over.

> An ethical dilemma is a situation that demands we make a choice about what is the right thing to do. If we want to be people who value the qualities of good character, then we must take the time to sort out these ethical dilemmas carefully.

Three Foundations for Ethical Decision Making

1. Take into account the interests and well-being of everyone concerned. (Don't do something that will help you if it will hurt another.)
2. When a character value like integrity and trustworthiness is at stake, always make the decision that will support that value. (For example, tell the truth even though it may cost you embarrassment—or even put you at risk in some way.)
3. Where two character values conflict (for instance, when telling the truth might hurt another person), choose the course of action that will lead to the greatest good for everyone concerned. Be sure to seek all possible alternatives, however; don't opt for dishonesty simply as the easiest and least painful way out of a difficult situation.

Robert Ho stayed behind to search for the baby. But he knew the building was in danger of collapsing any second. If he stayed any longer, his own children might lose their father. His family needed him; they trusted him to be there and provide for their needs. Besides, he was scared, and he wanted to get out of the building.

Robert was faced with an ethical dilemma. He could tell himself that two minutes either way wouldn't make any difference when it came to saving the baby's life. In fact, the baby might very well be dead already from smoke inhalation. No one, even the baby's mother, would expect him to risk his life if the situation were clearly hopeless, he told himself. But was he assessing the situation honestly? Was his fear making him avoid the truth? He couldn't hesitate; he had to make a decision now.

What would you do in this situation if you were the firefighter in that burning building? Would you do the right thing? How would you be sure what the right thing was?

If he were truthful with himself, Robert realized, he had at least two more minutes before the danger became critical. He paused only for a split second—and then he kept searching for that baby. About a minute later he found her crying inside her crib in another bedroom. He scooped her up and made it out of the burning building before it collapsed. The small breathing body in his arms and the look on her mother's face told him he had made the right decision.

Truth is more than a mental exercise.

—Thurgood Marshall

A firefighter's respect and compassion for others may ask him to take risks.

RESPECT AND COMPASSION

Sometimes respecting others means you'll need to take a risk....

CHAPTER THREE

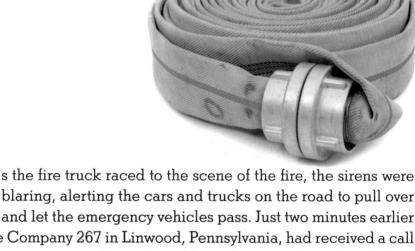

As the fire truck raced to the scene of the fire, the sirens were blaring, alerting the cars and trucks on the road to pull over and let the emergency vehicles pass. Just two minutes earlier Engine Company 267 in Linwood, Pennsylvania, had received a call from the emergency dispatcher. A house was on fire and neighbors were trying frantically to fight the blaze using a few garden hoses. "Hurry!" shouted the dispatcher. "There are reports that a pregnant woman and her pets might still be trapped inside!"

The fire-fighting squad that evening at Engine Company 267 consisted of the chief and eight firefighters. Seven of the firefighters had ten or more years' experience battling fires, but one of the crew, Barb Johnson, had been working with Engine Company 267 for only

At a fire a firefighter adjusts the flow rate on the hose lines.

Holding the nozzle steady requires physical strength.

a few months. During that time she had not seen as much action as the chief had hoped, but he knew it was only a matter of time before

the rookie's "baptism by fire" would take place. The chief had a hunch that tonight's fire might prove if the new recruit had "the right stuff." He was worried, though, that her inexperience could lead to disaster.

As the fire truck pulled up in front of the house, the firefighters quickly sprang into action. Two firefighters immediately sprayed the house with water

Rushworth M. Kidder, author of *How Good People Make Tough Choices*, writes that people often use three principles for resolving tough dilemmas like the one the chief faced. These principles are:

1. Do what others want you to do.
2. Do what's best for the greatest number of people.
3. Follow your highest sense of what is right.

Which of these principles do you think the chief used to reach his decision?

as the chief assessed the situation. The neighbors had turned off their garden hoses and retreated safely away from the scene. One of the neighbors ran up to the captain, screaming that the pregnant woman was still in the house.

"Let me go in!" Barb shouted to the chief.

The chief hesitated. He wanted to put this fire out quickly. He didn't want to risk the pregnant woman's life, nor did he want to endanger the rest of the crew by chancing that Barb might make a mistake. But he also understood Barb's need to prove herself. He respected her enough to take the risk. After all, a firefighter can only gain experience by fighting fires. "It's time," the chief agreed. "Don't forget everything you learned in training!"

The chief sent Barb and another firefighter into the burning house, along with a two-person hose crew. Together they entered the raging fire; the hoses sprayed the fire back with high-pressure water while Barb and the other crew member searched for the woman. Inside the smoky house, visibility was at zero percent. Barb kept one hand on the boot of the man in front of her and the other hand on the hose that snaked alongside her. The glimmer of the

Firefighters often face conditions where visibility is poor.

At every fire scene, the firefighter in charge has to make ethical decisions. Sometimes those decisions are hard, while other times they are easy to make. The chief might have used these five steps to help him reach his decision.

1. Recognize that there is a moral issue at hand. This is sometimes the hardest step for people to take. It may seem easier to ignore a problem and hope that it goes away by itself. But problems cannot be ignored; they must be dealt with. In this situation, the chief knew he was personally responsible for the safety of his fire crew—and this meant he had to make sure each crew member was working together at full capacity.

2. Evaluate the situation. In this situation, the chief had to quickly evaluate the fire scene and determine the best way to handle it. He had to immediately weigh all the options, including sending in the rookie as part of the rescue team. He knew he must make the right decision the first time because people's lives and property were at risk.

3. Decide. Firefighters are faced with many difficult decisions throughout their career, and they quickly learn how to make a decision. After the chief had carefully and quickly evaluated the situation, he made his decision and moved forward.

4. Implement. A firefighter can't ignore a problem, especially when it comes to making the right decision at a fire scene. In this case, the chief had made his decision and was trusting that the rookie and the other members of the rescue crew would save the woman and put out the fire.

5. Monitor and modify. Even though the chief had made his decision, he still had to stay in control of the situation. Firefighters keep in touch with their chief and each other via radios that are installed in their face masks. As the seconds turned into minutes, the chief was hearing a play-by-play commentary by the rescue team inside the house. If something had happened—for example, if there was an explosion inside the house, or if any of the firefighters had become injured—then the chief would have had to modify his original instructions. However, in this case it was not necessary.

After a fire, firefighters enjoy a chance to relax together and share a meal.

reflective stripes on the other firefighters' gear was the only way she could orient herself visually. She was frightened . . . but determined not to let her crew down.

Within a few minutes Barb and the other crewmember had located the pregnant woman and her cat and dog. Everyone was safely carried out of the house, and ten minutes later the fire was declared under control. Barb gave the chief a tired but grateful smile. "Thank you," she said quietly as he walked past her. She knew he understood.

[Compassion] builds. It is positive and helpful.
—Mary McLeod Bethune

When a firefighter enters a burning building, his sense of justice and fairness may ask him to endanger his own life for others.

JUSTICE AND FAIRNESS

You can't be a person of character only within your own group. Justice and fairness demand you act with the same strong character on behalf of everyone.

CHAPTER FOUR

On September 11, 2001, two planes were purposely crashed into the World Trade Center Twin Towers. People ran from the buildings as fire exploded through the floors. But firefighters rushed toward the disaster. More than 300 of them were killed trying to save innocent people who worked in those buildings. Many of those firefighters were supposed to be ending their shift and could have gone home; instead, they chose to rush to the scene with their fellow firefighters to do an enormous job. They felt the need to put themselves in harm's way to save innocent lives.

Since then, psychologists and mental health experts have studied the personalities of firefighters from engine companies everywhere. These researchers wanted to find out what makes a firefighter rush into a burning building without hesitating. What they found is that most people who become firefighters are a unique breed. "They are heroes and people who will do anything to help their fellow man," wrote one psychologist after interviewing hundreds of firefighters.

He and other mental health experts discovered that people who choose fire fighting as a career are action oriented and don't hesitate to take initiative quickly. That is evident to anyone who witnesses what takes place when a fire engine rolls onto an emergency scene. Firefighters know they have a job to do and they want to do that job to the best of their ability. They are team players who work together for a common goal. Firefighters know they need to take care of each other in order to get a dangerous job done. They also have a unique sense of justice and fairness, and tend to treat everyone with that attitude in mind.

According to a recent edition of the *Jobs Rated Almanac*, a reference guide published by the *Wall Street Journal*, fire fighting is

Firefighters are team players who work together as one unit.

Firefighters have a role to play after earthquakes or other disasters.

the second most stressful job after being president or prime minister. Most firefighters do not think about their jobs as being stressful, however. Firefighters know they are entering a dangerous situation—such as a burning building—and they simply focus on the job at hand. They do what they would want others to do for them. They are impelled to action by their strong sense of what is fair and just.

Firefighters have to be willing to work as hard for strangers as they would for their own families. They must see each individual life as uniquely valuable. No one can be dismissed as not being worthy of the firefighters' utmost efforts, and firefighters must be careful they don't seek their own safety while endangering the lives of others. Rather than pursuing the limelight

People who value justice and fairness treat all people the same (as much as possible). They consider carefully before making decisions that affect others. They cooperate with others and recognize the uniqueness and value of each individual.

In the midst of a fire, a firefighter takes a moment to suck in clean air.

Excuses We Make for Unethical Behavior

- If it's "necessary" then it's the right thing to do. The ends do not justify the means.
- If it's legal, it's okay. The law sets only a minimal standard of behavior; being unkind, telling a lie to a friend, or taking more than your share of dessert are not crimes—but they are still unethical.
- I was just doing it for you. Sometimes we tell "white lies" or evade the truth to avoid hurting another's feelings—when in fact, although the truth may be uncomfortable, it will do the other person good to hear it.
- I'm just fighting fire with fire; everybody does it. The behavior of those around you does not excuse your lack of fairness or other unethical behaviors. In cases like these, there is no safety in numbers!
- It doesn't hurt anyone. We often underestimate the cost of failing to do the right thing.
- It's okay so long as I don't gain personally. Although our actions may help some individuals, other individuals—including ourselves—are sure to suffer as a consequence of our unethical behavior.
- I've got it coming; I deserve to take more than my share because I worked more than anyone else. The Golden Rule applies here: would you want others to behave the same way?

Adapted from materials from the Josephson Institute of Ethics, josephsoninstitute.org/

as individuals, their sense of justice and fairness inspires them to work together smoothly as a team.

The brave firefighters who rushed to the scene of the World Trade Center Twin Towers on that fateful September day will always be remembered as heroes. News accounts tell many stories, like elevator mechanic Bobby Graff who remembers who saved his life that day: "Tall firefighters with the numbers 118 on their helmets." He was referring to Ladder 118's many brave firefighters who helped hundreds of people to safety that day. Ladder 118 Company had raced to the scene all the way from Brooklyn Heights, in another borough of the city.

If you are considering a career as a firefighter, how do you think you would react to a tragedy as enormous as the one that took place on September 11th? Do you feel such a strong sense of justice and fairness that you would want to be included in the rescue efforts—even if your job was in a different part of the city? Would you care more about others' equal rights to your protection, regardless of their location, than you would your own safety?

Choosing a career as a firefighter can mean many changes in your life. When the alarm sounds, you will have to scramble into your heavy coat, helmet, boots, and other lifesaving equipment and rush to an emergency scene. There you may be called on to put the rights of others ahead of your own well-being. Firefighters have a serious job to do. Make sure you are serious about your career choice; tackle it with a passion and enthusiasm; be fair and just to everyone.

And you will succeed.

Our aim must be to create a world of fellowship and justice. . . . "Love thy neighbor" is a precept which could transform the world if it were universally practiced.

—Mary McLeod Bethune

Firefighters have a long history of responsibility and dedication.

RESPONSIBILITY

*If you're a responsible person, you'll
never settle for second best when it
comes to helping others.*

CHAPTER FIVE

A devastating fire struck the city of Boston in 1711. It would influence fire fighting in America for years to come.

The fire started at about seven o'clock in the evening and quickly spread until it was out of control. The city of Boston had been suffering from drought conditions and over the next six or seven hours several hundred homes were destroyed. The Post Office and Town House were also engulfed in flames and burned completely to the ground.

Several heroic seamen tried in vain to save the bell that hung in the Old Meeting House before the fire spread there, but before they reached the bell, the roof collapsed. The seamen were killed. Dozens of other people were also lost trying to battle the blaze, which history records as one of the most devastating ever to strike the Colonies. Over a hundred families were left homeless, a dozen businesses were destroyed, and several city landmarks were ruined beyond recognition. The fire forced the city of Boston to start looking into a better system of fighting fires.

That fire in 1711 had a great impact on a six-year-old boy who witnessed the blaze for several hours. His name was Benjamin Franklin.

When Ben Franklin was 18 years old, he left Boston and traveled to Philadelphia to take up residence there. A few years later Philadelphia suffered a major fire disaster when fire broke out at the Fishbourne Wharf area. It caused considerable damage and several lives were lost. When the city had recovered from the tragic fire, the city officials realized they needed to take action to deal with any fires that might happen in the future. They recognized they needed better fire-fighting equipment, so they sent for two brand new fire engines from England. In addition, they ordered 400 leather buckets, 20 ladders, and 25 hooks. The city officials knew it was time to take responsibility and do something positive about fighting fires in and around Philadelphia.

Ben Franklin observed what the city had done, and in a newspaper he published he wrote editorials praising the city for their efforts. He used the newspaper as a way to advise the readers on how they could prevent fires. A few years later, however, he took on more responsibility for the city's fire-fighting efforts. In 1736, after a big fire broke out, he formed a *bucket brigade* that would respond to fires anywhere in the vicinity of the city. He wrote an article in his newspaper and asked for volunteers to help him with his new bucket brigade.

Ben Franklin was surprised when some 30 responsible people answered his call for help. It was at that moment in history that the first volunteer fire department was formed. Franklin called it the Union Fire Company, and word of their endeavors and success quickly spread throughout the city and across the state.

A Definition

Being **responsible** means you do your best, no matter what. Your behavior shows others you can be trusted. People will come to count on you, because they know you don't make excuses, you accept the consequences of your actions, and you always consider others' needs as well as your own.

Like the city officials, Franklin was being responsible. He did not care that forming the volunteer fire brigade was a difficult task. He saw a need and he responded with the appropriate action.

His idea became so popular that dozens of new volunteers came out over the next few days. Franklin didn't feel he needed more than 30 or 40 men in his fire company, so he urged the other volunteers to start their own fire companies. Because of Ben Franklin's act of responsibility, the city of Philadelphia quickly saw new fire departments created. They went by many different names: the Fellowship Fire Company, the Hand-in-Hand, the Heart-in-Hand, and the Friendship Fire Company. These names express the deep sense of responsibility to one another that was being acted out by these volunteers. Together with Ben Franklin's Union Fire Company, the city of Philadelphia had a strong fire-fighting base and quickly became a model for other cities to follow. They were doing their best for their community—and their fellow citizens knew they could rely on the volunteers' responsible efforts.

About 70 percent of all firefighters are volunteers. Only cities and larger communities can afford professional firefighters.

52

Today's firefighters don't only put out house fires. They are also called to:

- automobile accidents
- forest fires
- explosions
- collapsed buildings
- airplane crashes
- medical emergencies
- disaster relief after a hurricane, tornado, or flood

In some stations, more than half of all calls are medical emergencies rather than fires. Sometimes, firefighters even help deliver babies!

But that responsibility didn't stop with merely forming the new volunteer fire departments. These brave and dedicated men had to provide all their equipment at their own expense. They purchased fire engines, ladders, hooks, buckets, and other equipment as they could afford it.

All Ben Franklin's actions took place because he felt a sense of

Benjamin Franklin, patriot, inventor—and the founder of volunteer fire departments in America.

Early firefighters also had to provide the "siren" to alert neighborhoods.

obligation to the people of the city of Philadelphia. The memory of the tragic fire in Boston had stayed with him through his adult years. And because of his feeling of responsibility, Franklin created a system of volunteer firefighters that would grow and eventually reach every state in the country. Today firefighters, both volunteers and professionals, continue to risk their lives to save the lives and property of others.

Like Ben Franklin, you too have had many experiences that will stay in your memory throughout your life. Make good use of these memories, whether they are good

A standard of excellence is like a line you draw across your life. That line becomes your end goal in everything you do. You keep your eyes on it, and work hard to reach it.

What is that line? It's your personal best in any situation.

or bad. Allow them to move you forward in life; use them to build a foundation of good character, so that others will know they can count on you.

Today most fire departments have their own mission and values statement. This one is from the International Association of Firefighters Local 2719 in Centralia, Washington.

We, the professional firefighters of Local 2719 of the International Association of Firefighters, dedicate our efforts to provide for the safety and welfare of our community through the preservation of life, property and the environment. We seek opportunities to work cooperatively with labor and management to provide cost-effective, high quality emergency services while ensuring and improving the safety and benefits for our members.

It is the responsibility of each member to support this mission by subscribing to the following values:

FOR THE COMMUNITY
We recognize that the community is the reason for our existence.
All members of the public are entitled to our best efforts.
We will provide professional and courteous service at all times.
We value the faith and trust of the community and continually work to serve that confidence through our attitude, conduct and accomplishments.

FOR THE DEPARTMENT
We strive for excellence in everything we do.
Honesty, fairness and integrity will not be compromised.
We continually seek effectiveness, efficiency in economy, unity and teamwork that are stressed as being to our mutual advantage as individuals and employees.
The free exchange of ideas is encouraged.

Early fire engines were moved by manpower.

Famous Americans Who Served as Volunteer Firefighters

George Washington
Thomas Jefferson
Benjamin Franklin
Samuel Adams
Paul Revere
John Hancock
Alexander Hamilton
John Jay
Aaron Burr
John Barry

It's never too early to start acting responsibly. You can choose now to always take responsibility for your actions. Set yourself a standard of excellence. When you do, you are setting the framework for your future career. No matter what occupation you end up choosing, who knows what you will accomplish?

Nothing ever comes to one that is worth having, except as a result of hard work.

—Booker T. Washington

In the midst of an industrial fire, the hose crew uses a hand signal to call for more pressure.

COURAGE

Real courage seldom shows off.

CHAPTER SIX

Minutes after the first plane had crashed into the World Trade Center Tower dozens of fire companies began responding to the emergency alarms. Those brave men and women would end up facing the biggest challenge they had ever faced. Yet not one of them hesitated for even a second; they all responded with the courage and dedication required of all firefighters.

As the first fire engines pulled up in front of the World Trade Center Tower, the firefighters sprang into action and began the long journey up more than 80 floors. They knew it would take some time to haul the hoses, fire-fighting equipment, and *breaking gear* on their backs, but they were ready. As they began racing up the fire es-

A Definition

Courage means you answer others' call for help, even when your own safety may be at risk. It means you'll take on tasks no one else wants to tackle, and you stand up for what you believe.

capes, they soon were passing hundreds of office workers who were trying to get outside to safety.

The firefighters stopped for a few seconds about every 12 floors to catch their breath before continuing on their heroic journey. Many of the passing office workers poured bottled water over the firefighters to cool them off. "We knew they must be hot with all the equipment they were carrying and the fact that they were having to race up so many stairs," said one observer after he had made it to safety.

History will forever remember the heroic and courageous efforts made by hundreds of firefighters when the terrorist attacks took place on September 11, 2001. Firefighters from all across New York City responded to the sound of the emergency calls and did what they do best: they fought fires and rescued people. Without any concern for their own safety, they continued fighting until they could not fight anymore. Many firefighters' lives were lost that day.

After the terrorist attacks on September 11th, leaders from all over the world praised both firefighters and police for the heroic jobs they did during that terrible tragedy. British Prime Minister Tony Blair said in a tribute a few days after the attack, "Never forget the guts of the firefighters and police who died trying to save others."

Immediately following the attacks, then New York Mayor Rudolph Guiliani traded his suit and tie for hats and windbreakers bearing the logos of the fire and police departments. And celebrities from rock star Paul McCartney to Yankees manager Joe Torre took to wearing the FDNY (Fire Department of New York) logo.

Firefighters check their gear carefully between fires. Their safety and their ability to do their jobs well depend on their clothing and equipment.

The courageous firefighters from Engine 33/Ladder 9 in the city's Bowery section lost ten of their fire crew that day in September. In a newspaper article, Andy Morawek reported: "There's nothing that can describe it. It's hard to explain what you feel." That fire company lost 20 percent of their roster, and the survivors will never forget the courage that everyone showed in the face of so much danger. "They fought the good fight and never gave up," said another firefighter to reporters.

Story after story has been told of the courage that was demonstrated that day by firefighters. Joseph Graziano of Ladder 13 and Bill Casey of Engine 21 helped carry out an injured man. They kept telling the man that

In smoke-filled air, firefighters use self-contained breathing apparatus (SCBA). This includes a 25-pound tank of oxygen (carried on the firefighter's back) and a facemask. The mask leaves the ears uncovered, since hearing is especially important when vision is often obscured by smoke.

Special suits provide firefighters with protection from hazard-ous materials.

they would not abandon him and that they would keep going until he got out of the building safely. They got him out one minute before the building came crashing down.

Other firefighters kept the line of people moving safely out of the building. People were trying to stay calm, but it was difficult with so much chaos and pandemonium. One anonymous firefighter was seen telling people to keep moving. "People were starting to stop and stare at some of the bodies," an eyewitness told news reporters. "That brave firefighter kept encouraging and telling people to keep moving in an orderly fashion and no doubt saved hundreds of lives that day."

Those firefighters in New York City showed the world their cour-age. They answered the call to help, and many went above and be-yond the call of duty. They gave their lives to help others.

Over the last 20 years, an average of a hundred firefighters have died each year in the line of duty all across the country. But those losses suffered on September 11th were horrific and staggering:

more than 300, nearly 30 times the number ever lost by any fire department in a single fire-fighting event, have been listed as missing or dead. But despite the large numbers of firefighters who were injured or who lost their lives that day, firefighters have become the heroes of today's world. Early signs indicate fire fighting may become the trendy job of tomorrow.

Florida State Fire College and other fire training schools around the country have seen twice as many applicants since the terrorist attacks. Many people are feeling a sense of obligation to become firefighters. But not everyone is cut out for a career in fire fighting. No matter how prestigious fire fighting may be right now, not everyone can do this difficult and dangerous job. If you are considering a career as a firefighter, you need to learn as much as you can about the job requirements and the various scenarios you might encounter in that field.

Many people mistakenly think that courage is something they can brag about. They connect courage with being a daredevil to impress others. But in the fire-fighting profession, courage is something that is simply expected, not something to be put on display.

Climbing a ladder into a fire demands great bravery.

The Difference Between Physical and Moral Courage

Physical courage means you do what needs doing, even when it puts you physically in danger. Physical courage asks that you risk bodily injury or even death.

Moral courage means you stand up for what is right, no matter the financial, social, or emotional cost to yourself. You resist pressure from your peers to do something you know is wrong. You act with character even when you are the only one to do so.

Which do you think is more difficult?

Facing the thick smoke and fire caused by a petroleum fire requires both physical and moral courage.

Firefighters draw courage from one another.

True heroes who exhibit courage are usually surprised when other people view them as heroes. Instead, they simply view what they are doing as part of their job, and they do that job to the best of their ability, no matter what dangers or problems they encounter along the way.

In the face of danger, *camaraderie* is a powerful motivator to help firefighters find the courage they need to do those jobs. Dennis Smith, author of *Report from Engine Co. 82*, writes "In the department, you're presented with a collective memory of the many people who lost their lives in the course of duty before you. Then, as you go forward, you feel more and more that you are a part of this great

Being a Daredevil vs. a Person of Courage

A daredevil takes risks to impress others.

A daredevil gets "high" on the adrenaline rush caused by danger.

A person of courage acts on behalf of others even if she is afraid.

A person of courage stands up for what is right even when he stands alone.

tradition of brave people. That collective memory is the thing that inspires firefighters to continue, even after a great, great disaster like the one that took place on September 11th."

In other words, we can draw courage from each other. You'll find this is true as well in life outside the fire-fighting world. Look around at the people in your life who are truly brave. Follow their footsteps. Take courage from their example.

Of course, courage alone is not always enough. People who choose fire fighting as a career have a personal responsibility to ensure that they are physically and mentally prepared to answer the call. They must be able to achieve excellence in all they do. But above all, they must have the courage to act—and that courage involves not only physical courage but moral courage as well.

If you are considering a career in fire fighting, one way you can prepare yourself is to seek the answer to this question: How can you live courageously today?

You can make it. Hold your head high, stick your chest out. You can make it. It gets dark sometimes, but the morning comes. Don't you surrender.

—Jesse Jackson

A fire-fighting boat uses a hose mounted on a deck gun.

SELF-DISCIPLINE AND DILIGENCE

Never, ever give up!

CHAPTER SEVEN

S elf-discipline and diligence are two character traits that every firefighter must have. From the time they start training until they graduate and become official firefighters, whether volunteer or paid, those brave men and women know that they must never give up. Winston Churchill, a world leader from Great Britain during World War II, was famous for saying "never give up, never give up, never, ever, give up!" And that motto has been adopted by fire-fighting training schools all around the world.

Men and women who enlist in the United States Navy are all required to be trained as firefighters. They attend fire training schools, which are located on numerous Naval bases throughout the coun-

Firefighters on board a ship need the same self-discipline and diligence any firefighter does.

try. Every crew member on a Navy ship needs to know how to fight fires, because if a fire breaks out while a ship is in the middle of the ocean, there are no fire departments to contact. Instead, each member of the crew is responsible for one or more assignments on the Fire Control Team. Every person on board a ship knows that the deadliest enemy they may encounter is fire, and they want to be prepared.

On a recent Monday morning at the Norfolk Naval Base in Virginia, nearly 60 men and women reported for fire training school. Most of those sailors had only been on their ships for a few weeks, and they were now getting ready to learn critical fire-fighting skills that would help them become vital members of the ship's crew. The first few hours were spent in the classroom, where the instructors shared the basics of fire fighting.

After lunch came the time for actual

People who are self-disciplined and diligent keep going even when the going is rough—and even when it's boring.

hands-on training, and the fire-fighting students gathered in groups of ten people. Several instructors showed them what their first task would be: to enter a burning building as a team and extinguish the fire. Each team was also

The Navy isn't the only place where you might work on water while being a firefighter. Some cities' fire-fighting crews also use boats. Other firefighters use helicopters and small airplanes, especially for battling forest fires.

assigned an experienced fire-fighting professional from the Navy. These professionals would not only see that the teams were following proper procedures, but they also made sure that no one was injured during the training sessions.

The buildings used for fire-fighting training were specially designed and built to withstand excessive heat and high temperatures. The training teams had to enter the building and climb several flights of stairs to fight the fires, which were actually contained in special areas. The fires could not spread beyond the confines of those areas, which made it easier to train fire-fighting crews and make sure everything was done safely.

The first few times were hectic and chaotic. The crews had to unroll hoses, attach special nozzles, and find the right equipment to battle the blazes. Despite the difficult task, every member of the training crews met the challenge. They knew that someday they might be called on to fight a fire aboard their ship, and they wanted to be prepared. It was hot and everyone was tired, but they had the self-discipline and diligence to keep on going. Never once did they even consider quitting. They had a job to do, and they did it well.

Those brave men and women who undergo the intense fire-fighting training graduate with honors at the end of the week. The program was designed to ensure that all those who leave the fire training school have enough experience to handle themselves in any fire-fighting situation on board a ship.

72

That training has saved many lives throughout Navy history—like the time a fire broke out on board the *aircraft carrier* the USS *Enterprise*. On January 14, 1969, at 8:19 in the morning, several explosions aboard the flight deck resulted in serious fires in several sections of the ship. As the fire alarm was sounded, everyone responded and manned the fire-fighting stations for which they had been trained.

At the time of the explosions, the *Enterprise* was 70 miles south of Pearl Harbor undergoing operational readiness inspection prior to deployment to Vietnam for the ship's fourth combat tour in the Western Pacific. Luckily, 90 percent of the seamen had attended fire-fighting schools in the past six months. The first assistance to arrive were the destroyers USS *Rogers* and USS *Stoddard*, which quickly came alongside to aid the hundreds of sailors manning the hoses on the flight deck. According to U.S. Navy reports, Navy, Marine, Coast Guard, and Air Force helicopters carried seriously wounded men to Tripler Army Hospital in Honolulu. But the fire

Forestry departments often use airplanes to combat forest fires.

Helicopters are often used for dropping water onto forest fires.

would have been even more disastrous without the diligence and self-discipline of the firefighters on board.

Another fire broke out on a Navy destroyer, the USS *Harlan R. Dickson*, that was stationed at the Boston Naval Station. This time a fire started in the engine room shortly after dinner on a Friday evening. Although many sailors had left the ship on leave and would be gone the entire weekend, the crew that was assigned to duty that day sprang into action. Within minutes they had the fire under control, and a short time later everything was back to normal.

In all the fires that took place on board dozens of Navy ships over the years, there was one common factor: the fire-fighting crews that responded to fight those fires did so with enthusiasm and

Being a firefighter is not always exciting. While on duty, many city firefighters have plenty of everyday opportunities to practice self-discipline and diligence. They have to do ordinary jobs like shopping, cooking, cleaning, paying bills, and taking care of equipment and uniforms.

a fervor that would make any fire training instructor proud. The combination of their dedication, along with the hours of training that they continued to practice, made those crews able to handle themselves in the time of need. Their self-discipline and diligence not only saved their own lives but the lives of their fellow crew.

How about you? Are you ready to work hard to become a fire-fighting professional? Do you think you have the self-discipline and diligence necessary?

Ask yourself these questions:

Am I the type of person who can set goals and work toward completing them, no matter how many obstacles might get in my way?
Am I the type of person who is willing to forgo my own pleasure and immediate gratification for the greater good?
Am I the type of person who can set limits and boundaries?

If you answered yes to those questions, then you are exhibiting an important element of good character: self-discipline and diligence.

As long as I can . . . I'll keep on keeping on.

—Ray Charles

A tired firefighter enjoys a glass of water after doing his job to protect his community.

CITIZENSHIP

*If you're a good citizen, you don't only
care about what's good for
you—you also care about what's good for your
entire community.*

CHAPTER EIGHT

By now you have learned about some of the very important character traits that firefighters must have in order to do their jobs. Citizenship is another important character trait that firefighters must always strive to possess. This quality not only means being a law-abiding citizen, but it also means that you should become involved in some type of service to your community and country. It's the quality that links you directly with others. Firefighters work as members of a team, and it is extremely important that each and every member of that team support and look out for each other. But they don't only take care of each other; and they don't only help deal with fires and other disasters. They also do what they can to make their communities better places for everyone.

Fire stations' mascots are a way to form community ties, particularly with the younger members of the community.

There are thousands of examples from all over the country where firefighters have become involved in community service projects. One such example has taken place in Michigan, where the Big Brothers of Greater Muskegon (now Big Brothers Big Sisters of the Lakeshore), have a program that links young students with firefighters. Known as the Face to Face Program, it connects young boys in need of a role model with mentors from their neighborhood fire station. Firefighters are effective models for these youth between the ages of 11 and 15. While at the fire station, the boys work on self-paced, character-enriching workbooks, and the firefighters assist the boys if they have questions.

During the six-week program, the Little Brother visits the firehouse on a weekly basis, for a two-hour block of time. Following the hands-on time spent with the workbooks, the boys and the firefighters are free to interact on a more personal level. Whether they choose to shoot hoops (and learn the character quality of fairness), snack on pizza (and learn responsibility as they clean up afterward), or just hang out and watch television, the boys will have many chances to apply what they have learned about character. Trustworthiness,

After a train derailed and struck a factory building, firefighters turned out to do their part.

What Is Good Citizenship?

According to the Character Counts Coalition, citizenship includes all these behaviors:

- Playing by the rules
- Obeying the law
- Doing your share
- Respecting authority
- Keeping informed about current events
- Voting
- Protecting your neighbors and community
- Paying your taxes
- Giving to others in your community who are in need
- Volunteering to help
- Protecting the environment
- Conserving natural resources for the future

respect, fairness, caring, responsibility, and good citizenship may just be words in the beginning, but the boys will learn how to apply these character traits in their everyday lives.

Several of the boys who have been through the program have had an opportunity to ride along on one of the fire engines. This chance of a lifetime depends on the firefighters and the fire station's policy. Not all stations offer this opportunity, but the choice is always left to the discretion of the firefighters.

Many of the firefighters that have been involved with this program have signed up to do it again as often as they could because they see the changes in the youth. "It is a good feeling to watch these young people learn responsibility and what it means to practice good citizenship," said one firefighter.

You're never too young to begin practicing good citizenship. Each time you do your share to help out in your community, you are being a good citizen. As you make citizenship a habit, you will be laying a solid foundation for your future profession.

No one does it alone.

—Oprah Winfrey

The fire alarm box means that somewhere a crew of firefighters is ready to do their job.

CAREER OPPORTUNITIES

*Good character is an asset that will
help you achieve ... now and in the future.*

CHAPTER NINE

I f you decide on a career in the fire-fighting field, you will have a big responsibility. You will be helping people by saving their lives and property, and by protecting communities and ensuring that everyone enjoys a better quality of life.

In the year 2010, there were about 310,400 jobs. Besides fire-fighters, other people who worked in the fire prevention industry include first-line supervisors/managers of fire fighting, prevention workers, and fire inspectors. In addition to paid career firefighters, there are thousands of volunteers, both men and women, who donate their time to fight fires in their local communities. In fact, about 70 percent of all firefighters are volunteers.

Professional firefighters may be employed by cities, counties, or even states.

Some large cities have thousands of career firefighters, while many small towns have only a few. Most of the remainder work in fire departments on federal and state installations, including airports. Private fire-fighting companies employ a small number of firefighters and usually operate on a *subscription basis*.

In response to the expanding role of firefighters, some municipalities have combined fire prevention, public fire education, safety, and emergency medical services into a single organization, often referred to as a public safety organization. Some local and regional fire departments are being consolidated into countywide establishments in order to reduce administrative staffs and cut costs, and to establish consistent training standards and work procedures.

Prospective firefighters are expected to face keen competition for available job openings. Many people are attracted to fire fighting because it is challenging and provides the opportunity to perform an essential public service, a high school education is usually

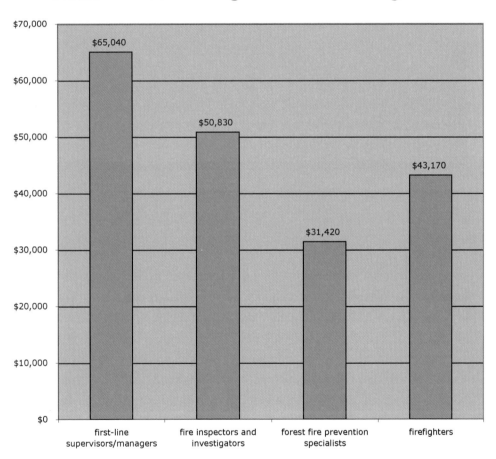

Median Annual Earnings in 2007 for Firefighters

Fire fighting is an essential service in every community and region.

sufficient for entry, and a pension is guaranteed upon retirement after 20 years. Consequently, the number of qualified applicants in most areas exceeds the number of job openings, even though the written examination and physical requirements eliminate many applicants. This situation is expected to persist in coming years.

Employment of firefighters is expected to increase more slowly than the average for all occupations through 2020 as fire departments continue to compete with other public safety providers for funding. Most job growth will occur as volunteer fire-fighting positions are converted to paid positions. In addition to job growth, openings are expected to result from the need to replace firefighters who retire, stop working for other reasons, or transfer to other occupations.

The first known woman firefighter was an African American woman named Molly Williams, who took her place in 1818 with the men as she pulled the pumper through the deep snow to put out a fire.

The firefighter's badge, the Maltese Cross, has a tradition that is hundreds of years old.

When a courageous band of Crusaders, known as the Knights of St. John, fought the Saracens for possession of the Holy Land, they encountered a new weapon unknown to European warriors. The Saracens' weapon was fire.

As the Crusaders advanced on the walls of the Saracens' city they were struck by glass bombs containing naphtha. When they became saturated with the highly flammable liquid, the Saracens hurled a flaming tree into their midst. Hundreds of Knights were burned alive. Others risked their lives to save their brothers-in-arms from dying painful fiery deaths.

These men became the first firefighters. Their heroism was recognized by fellow Crusaders, who awarded each hero a badge of honor, a cross similar to the one firefighters wear today. Since the Knights of John lived for almost four centuries on a little island in the Mediterranean Sea named Malta, the cross came to be known as the Maltese Cross.

The Maltese Cross means that the firefighter who wears it is willing to lay down his or her life for others. It is a firefighter's badge of honor, signifying that he or she works with all the qualities essential to a person of good character.

Adapted from the FDNY website:www.nyc.gov/html/fdny/html/history/maltese_cross.shtml

Layoffs of firefighters are uncommon. Fire protection is an essential service, and citizens are likely to exert considerable pressure on local officials to expand or at least preserve the existing level of fire protection. Even when budget cuts do occur, local fire departments usually reduce expenses by postponing equipment purchases or not hiring new firefighters, rather than by laying off staff. Fire

The Dragon Slayers, Aniak, Alaska's all-girl rescue crew, prove that women can be strong firefighters of character. The girls are all 15 to 19 years old (they're not allowed to enter burning buildings until they're 18), and they operate pumper trucks; drag 70-pound, 50-foot hoses; read cardiac monitors; and fly with medevac pilots. They complete 100 hours of training before they go on calls, and put in another 140 hours of training after they begin as Dragon Slayers.

Being a firefighter has made a big difference to each of these girls. "Now I know I can do anything," says Mariah Brown, one of the Dragon Slayers, "especially when people think I can't. I just say, 'Watch me.'"

The cross worn by the Knights of the Cross during the Crusades evolved into today's firefighters' emblem.

Firefighters have the opportunity to make a positive difference in our world.

fighting involves hazardous conditions and long, irregular hours, but because this type of a career offers job security and the opportunity to perform an essential public service, competition is high.

Fire-fighting careers for women have an excellent outlook for the future. According to the International Association of Women in Fire and Emergency Services, around 62,000 women are currently working as full-time, career firefighters and officers. They also estimate that around 35,000 women are in the volunteer fire service in the United States. Although most people think of men when they think of firefighters who rush into burning buildings, the number of women firefighters has been slowly increasing over the past 25 to 30 to 40 years.

If you are interested in a career as a firefighter, you can look forward to advancements and salary increases if you work hard at your profession. But most important, as a firefighter, you have the power to make a difference in the world. You can make the world a safer place in which to live. You will do this by choosing the core qualities of a good character:

- integrity and trustworthiness
- respect and compassion
- justice and fairness
- responsibility
- courage
- self-discipline and diligence
- citizenship

Good character is an asset—one that will help you go far in whatever career you choose.

There is so much to be done, and we are the ones to get it done. You can play a role in your community.

—Colin Powell

Further Reading

Josephson, Michael S. and Wes Hanson, editors. *The Power of Character*. Bloomington, Ind.: Unlimited Publishing, 2004.

Kidder, Rushworth M. *How Good People Make Tough Choices*. New York: HarperCollins, 2009.

Learning Express Editors. *Becoming a Firefighter: Finding and Getting a Rewarding Job*. New York: LearningExpress, 2008.

Oleksy, Walter G. *Choosing a Career as a Firefighter*. New York: Rosen Publishing Group, 2000.

Smith, Bob. *Becoming a Firefighter: The Complete Guide to Your Badge!* San Jose, Calif.: Code 3 Publishing, 2003.

For More Information

Canada's Firefighting Portal
www.firefightingincanada.com

International Association of Firefighters
www.iaff.org

The New York City Fire Museum
www.nycfiremuseum.org

Center for the 4th and 5th Rs
www.cortland.edu/c4n5rs

Character Education Network
www.charactered.net

Publisher's Note:
The websites listed on this page were active at the time of publication. The publisher is not responsible for websites that have changed their address or discontinued operation since the date of publication. The publisher will review and update the websites upon each reprint.

Glossary

Aircraft carrier A warship with a flight deck where airplanes can be launched and landed.

Arson The crime of purposefully setting a fire.

Breaking gear Equipment used for cutting through walls and doors to get to trapped victims and reach fires.

Bucket brigade A line of people that quickly pass buckets of water from one to another.

Camaraderie A spirit of friendly fellowship.

Canine search teams Search units that use dogs specially trained to find victims after a disaster.

Dispatcher The person who takes and conveys the message that a fire has started and where.

Ethical dilemma A situation where a person is presented with a choice and must decide on the right course of action.

Halligan bar A firefighter's essential tool, it contains a claw, lever, and a cutting blade.

Hazardous materials units Teams that are trained to deal specifically with dangerous chemicals and other substances.

Initiative A character quality that means a person is willing to go ahead and take the first step, without waiting for anyone else.

Resilient When a person is able to emotionally bounce back after a crisis.

Subscription basis Something that you sign up to do.

Index

About the Authors & Consultants

John Riddle is the author of 15 books and a speaker and presenter at many writers' conferences around the country.

Rae Simons has written many novels and young adult nonfiction. She lives in New York State.

Cheryl Gholar is a Community and Economic Development Educator with the University of Illinois Extension. She has a Ph.D. in Educational Leadership and Policy Studies from Loyola University, and she has more than 20 years of experience with the Chicago Public Schools as a teacher, counselor, guidance coordinator, and administrator. Recognized for her expertise in the field of character education, Dr. Gholar assisted in developing the K–12 Character Education Curriculum for the Chicago Public Schools, and she is a five-year participant in the White House Conference on Character Building for a Democratic and Civil Society. The recipient of numerous awards, she is also the author of *Beyond Rhetric and Rainbows: A Journey to the Place Where Learning Lives.*

Ernestine G. Riggs is an Assistant Professor at Loyola University Chicago and a Senior Program Consultant for the North Central Regional Educational Laboratory. She has a Ph.D. in Educational Leadership and Policy Studies from Loyola University, and she has been involved in the field of education for more than 35 years. An advocate of teaching the whole child, she is a frequent presenter at district and national conferences; she also serves as a consultant for several state boards of education. Dr. Riggs has received many citations, including an award from the United States Department of Defense Overseas Schools for Outstanding Elementary Teacher of America.